Old Haxby & New Ears

Paul Chrystal

The Village, Haxby, looking west with the 1878 St. Mary's church on the right. This postcard by Valentine's of Dundee uses a 1905 photo but Haxby has become 'Hoxby'!

First published in the United Kingdom, 2015,
by Stenlake Publishing Ltd.
Telephone: 01290 551122
www.stenlake.co.uk

ISBN 9781840336894

Acknowledgements

Many people have been very kind and generous in their help with the content of this book and, in so doing, have improved it beyond all measure. They include Steve Lewis and Anne Wood at *The York Press* for allowing me unrestricted access to their archives, yet again (see the images on the inside front cover and on pages 4–12); Elaine Armstrong, Assistant Head and Director of Communications, The Joseph Rowntree School, New Earswick; and Mark Sessions, for permission to use some photos originally published by Sessions in Joe Murphy's *New Earswick - A Pictorial History*. Sue Everard has kindly provided some fascinating pictures of New Earswick life from the Joseph Rowntree Foundation Archive; they are on pages 21, 23, 24, 27, 35, 37, 39, 44–47. The image on page 19 was generously provided by Bill Fawcett and was originally published in his fascinating *George Townsend Andrews of York, the 'Railway Architect'* published by Yorkshire Architectural & York Archaeological Society and the North Eastern Railway Association. Thanks too to Sylvia Hall at Dutch Nurseries and Andrew Clarke at Northern Scientific for the information they provided regarding their businesses.

Left: Map showing Haxby and Strensall in 1720; there would be no New Earswick for another 180 years.

'Happy Haxby'

One of the earliest references to Haxby, in the 11th century, refers to it as Haxebi ("Hacca's Farm" in Norse). There is evidence of a Roman presence in the form of what was possibly a villa on Haxby Moor, pottery found in Station Road and a silver signet ring. A 9th century Viking settlement is indicated by the discovery of the base of a cross in St Mary's churchyard and in 1978 two large fragments of a 10th century Anglo-Scandinavian cross shaft with Celtic markings were found in the garden of 54 The Village. The cross is currently held by the York Archaeological Trust; perhaps it should be released to sit with the base that is in St Mary's church so that the people of Haxby can enjoy it? Flooding was an early village problem; as far back as the 16th century we hear "[the flooding] *was offentimes so urgent and grete that th'inhabitants ther about fore the space of a moneth and more could passe no whither for incumberns of the said water.*"

Haxby's entry in Domesday reads: "*6 carucates* (the amount of land ploughable in one season), *1 bovate taxable, 4 ploughs possible. St Peter* (i.e. the Minster) *had it and has it. There are 7 villagers and 3 ploughs. Value pre 1066, 20 shillings, now 10 shillings.*" The devaluation was a result of the depradation wreaked by William the Conqueror's Harrying of the North – his scorched earth campaign to subdue revolting northerners.

Up until the second half of the 20th century the 2,000 acres of the parish were almost totally devoted to agriculture. 1,100 acres were under cultivation and 800 as pasture at the time of enclosure in 1769. Parish registers from around 1850 show that of the 218 men recorded, 144 were farmers or farm labourers and a further 46 were in trades supporting farming, such as blacksmiths and carpenters. The *1941 Farm Survey* shows there to be no fewer than 38 farms in and around Haxby including many, like the 107 acre Church Farm at what is now 44 The Village, in the centre of the village itself.

Brick and tile making was the other main industry in Haxby with five different brick makers recorded in 1881, all exploiting the rich clay seam under Haxby's topsoil. They were concentrated in North Lane and on Usher Lane and behind York Road (nos. 103 and 105 where the brick ponds, now fishing lakes, can still be seen). The 1881 census shows eighteen people in Haxby in the brick and tile business, the most prominent of which were members of the Driffield family. The tiles were used in some of the village's late 19th century houses. The first evidence of brick manufacture is in the early 17th century when Haxby builders started using brick soon after the construction of a brick house in Ogleforth in York, after 1666. In the 18th century the terraced cottages beyond the Hospice shop were built of very small local bricks. There were four brick builders here in 1771. Locally made bricks are mainly small, pink, light brown or grey. The elegant terrace in York Road is made with white bricks, Scarborough Buff, which also come in yellow. They were built between 1902 and 1904 by Bert Prole at Driffield's brick yard in the village.

The first school in Haxby was where the Tiger is now; this was superseded by the 1851 school: The Church of England School "*for the children of the labouring poor of Haxby*" – 60 boys and eight girls. The staff comprised the Head, a sewing mistress and a pupil teacher; this is now St. Mary's Hall in North Lane. The Board School opened in 1876; it cost £2,200 and had 53 pupils on the roll. Early school governors seem to have been unduly strict if the day book for November 8th 1878 is anything to go by: "*The registers have not been marked since Monday for the following reason, viz on Tuesday members of the board...came to the school and with sticks violently drove the children, some out of the school, and others from getting in.*" The school is now the Memorial Hall, dedicated to the Haxby fallen in the World Wars: twenty-seven in the First World War (3% of the population) and nine in the Second World War. The clock was erected to commemorate the Coronation of Edward VII, the bill for which remained unpaid for two years due to administrative confusion. Plus ça change.

The first Methodist Chapel in Haxby opened in 1782 in North Lane, behind what is now the St Leonard's Hospice shop. In 1813 they moved to a new chapel in The Village, where the fish and chip shop stands today. In 1837 the first Primitive Methodist Chapel opened on the corner of Westfield Lane (right). Two years later in 1879 the present Methodist Chapel opened to serve Haxby and Wigginton. In 1932 the Wesleyan Methodist, Primitive Methodist and United Methodist churches all came together to form The Methodist Church in its new building.

In the 1930s the Primitive Methodist Chapel become vacant when the Methodist churches moved into a purpose built church further up the road towards Wigginton. Northern Scientific were established in this building in 1981, selling new, reconditioned and second hand vacuum equipment mainly to scientific and research laboratories in universities, hospitals, to DEFRA, and steel makers Tata. Their product lines include: vacuum pumps; vacuum gauges; vacuum fittings and vacuum oils (fomblin, mineral, silicone). In the interim it had been used for commercial storage and bought by NYCC to be converted into an ambulance station. When the new ambulance station opened in the mid 60s at the top of York Road, North Yorkshire County Council's Architect's Department moved their York area Buildings Maintenance offices into the building.

As the photo shows there were three front doors installed for the ambulance station; the right hand door has been retained. The company moved to Haxby from their offices in Blossom Street near the Odeon. It was bought at auction as 'The Former Ambulance Station' through auctioneers A. Stansfield & Son, New Street and R & D Kay, 66 The Village, Haxby. The front is faced with pilasters of orange machine-made bricks; side walls are English Garden Bell Bond – the most common brick in Haxby.

Home of the Finlandia Sauna in 1974, this building (built in 1838 as a private residence) is the one next to Haxby Shopping Centre.

The Dutch Nurseries as they were in 1974 with windmill precariously perched on the roof. Locals will know the work of Jacob Verhoef today from the beautiful flower displays which decorate the entrance to Haxby at the corner of Mill Lane.

Jacob arrived in Haxby in 1952 from a village near Aalsmeer in Holland intent on making a life for himself in horticulture. He started work for Hollandia Nurseries which was owned by Peter van Zelst, at the end of The Avenue off Sandy Lane; Hollandia were wholesale only, with shops in Davygate (on the site of Betty's Bar) and market stalls in Knaresborough, York and Ripon. Jacob lived in digs in Hilbra Avenue and then in Station Road; he bought the Hollandia cut flowers business and the market pitches in 1956 and registered the name 'Dutch Nurseries' – the first such registration in the U.K. To get more exposure, he bought the land between Moor Lane and the terraces which was occupied by allotments and a sand quarry used for filling sandbags; likewise, the land on the opposite corner across Moor Lane. Jacob then moved into retail, drained the soggy land (in true Dutch style), bought some greenhouses, built a shop and started selling pink carnations. The business blossomed and in 1988 the old shop was demolished and replaced with the building we see today – along with the chemist shop which Jacob saw as an opportunity – given the health centre straight over the road. Wyre Court and Birchlands Nursing Home occupy the rest of the land which Jacob had sold off. The Corporation gave him the 'freedom but not the right' to cultivate the land on the corner – hence the resplendent displays.

My thanks to Sylvia Hall of Dutch Nurseries for much of this information, and to Jacob Verhoef whose memories are published in *Haxby Dutchman's Diamond Jubilee 1952–2012* by Peter Stanhope.

Another 1970s shot of the village, this time showing the petrol station and garage in Station Road, now run by Pulleyn's. Foxton Ronald (Bill) Pulleyn started in the motor trade when he was fourteen; by the time he retired he had three garages: one on this site in Haxby which is still thriving under Richard Pulleyn, one in Wigginton (now gone and redeveloped as houses) and one on Wigginton Road which is now a Skoda dealer. The first of these opened in 1958. Behind the garage in Wigginton was a blacksmith's operated by Victor Pulleyn; Victor previously drove mule trains for the army in Mesopotamia (modern day Iraq) during the First World War; there were also a corn mill and steam engine there.

The Avenue, part of the Park Estate off York Road, in 1972 with a Ford Anglia negotiating the then unimproved private road. The Avenue was built in 1922 offering a range of architectural house styles. Builders on the site included Francis John Pulleyn, a Mr. Copley, Stanley Pulleyn and Verdun Pulleyn. John Pulleyn had started the building business and his son, Francis John, set up the family brickworks. The road was later developed at a cost of £4,000.

The opening of the swimming pool at Ralph Butterfield County Primary School in July 1964 by international swimmer Pauline Clarkson, from Haxby. Many comments on Facebook recall how cold it always was; this is typical: '*it was bloody freezing and so was the metal bucket you had to stand in before getting in the pool... oh yes and the outside changing rooms – complete with peep holes!*' The school is named after, and in honour of, Ralph Butterfield O.B.E., a prominent North Yorkshire educationalist who distinguished himself at Passchendaele where he won the Military Cross. The school was built on Sharp's Field, a football pitch named after William Sharp, a York pawnbroker, who had lived nearby at the Laurels; it educated 200 children in five classrooms. In 1970 the Usher Lane annexe was built; in 1974 this became Oaken Grove School, but it closed in 2002. In July 2014, pupils at the school helped to create a series of sculptures at the Coppergate Centre to mark the Tour De France's flash through York. Pupils wove old jumpers into recycled bike wheels to represent the four main colours of jersey worn by the category-winning riders. The wheels top off giant metal flowers which have been 'planted' in the shopping centre.

Robsons Eucomarket in 1979 – just one in a long line of supermarkets that have occupied this site in The Village. The Midland Bank and Finlandia Sauna are on the left. Robsons, which survived into the mid-1970s, was a Scarborough-based supermarket; the Haxby building was named Clarke House after Gordon Clarke, a builder who worked for Jim Pulleyn who built the arcade on the site of what was Bell's Garage. It would seem that the inconsiderate double-parking has long been a problem.

The Memorial Hall on the left in 1973, looking towards the roundabout and the unattractive building that is Haxby Hall – an example of civic vandalism where a perfectly fine building was replaced (in 1965) with the dullest construction imaginable – to serve as a home for 52 elderly people and ambulance station. The original Grade II listed building situated in 22 acres was built in 1790 and features on the front cover of this book. An unusual, striking feature was the glass cupola over the stairwell. Notwithstanding, it was demolished in 1963 despite local protests. It had started life as a private residence and was used up to 1853 as the Rev. John Heslop's Classical and Mathematical Academy for *"Sons of Gentlemen of high respectability; £50 p.a. including washing."* Apart from the usual maths, Latin and Greek, lessons included *"Navigation, the Use of Globes, and the Construction of Maps"*. In the Second World War it was requisitioned to accommodate evacuees from Hull and Middlesbrough as well as being the local First Aid centre and HQ for the ARP. In 1950 Kenneth Ward, the then owner, donated nine acres to the village which became the Ethel Ward Memorial Playing Field in honour of his late wife. This now comprises a scout hut, playground, football pitches and other facilities for the enjoyment of local residents. The Field was opened in 1948 by Maurice Leyland, England and Yorkshire cricketer.

The level crossing at the entrance to the village looking towards New Earswick, in 1965. The signal box was demolished in 1988.

Haxby Station, where Pulleyn's garage now is on Station Road, opened in 1845; it was closed to passengers in 1930 but remained open for freight and coal for some years after. Cargoes included boxes of fish, Lyons cakes, calves, animal feedstuffs, straw, grain and soldiers on the way to Strensall. *The York Herald* of 12th December 1864 carried a report of a fatal accident enquiry. Thomas Hawcroft, stationmaster at Haxby, had been run over by a wagon while trying to help his porter and later died after his foot had been amputated: *"his left foot was crushed in a shocking manner, the soft parts being very much torn."* Verdict: accidental killing.

This photograph from the mid 1990s shows the girls from Barbara Taylor's School of Dancing with their medals. Rachael Chrystal is third from the right on the front row. The school was in the Memorial Hall beyond which in the 1940s was Bryant's the grocer's and the houses which replaced the demolished cottages in what was called Younghusband's Row.

The Gothic style St. Mary's Church was built in 1878 and is on the site of the Chapel of Our Lady which had burned down. St. Mary's has a single bell on which *"fili dei miserere mei 1621"* is inscribed. The original church had no burial licence and there are stories of corpses being *"casually lost"* on the way to being buried at Strensall Church. This happened to Thomas Westeby, whose body, *"by reason of the great distance and the badness of the ways"* fell into the River Foss. The earlier chapel owned a number of properties for which the rent was payable in hens and eggs. Tom Holtby (Rash Tom), the last stagecoach driver on the Doncaster-York leg of the London-Edinburgh mail route, is buried here.

Station Road looking east towards the railway station. John Wright, an evacuee from Middlesbrough, gives an intriguing account of Haxby during the Second World War in his *An Evacuee's Story*. He was 'billeted' at 66 York Road with two spinsters and describes life there and at the school which is now the Memorial Hall. The house, the original Haxby Hall, the orchards behind the terraces on York Road and the area known as the Headlands (where the plough horses turned) with its tennis courts are all described in some detail. Haxby's Headlands School is named after this area.

York Road in July 2014 – the house where John Wright lived as an evacuee is second from the right.

The roundabout, looking west towards what is now the Memorial Hall on the right with St. Mary's beyond that. Widd's Farm was where Westow House is now on the near left – it was originally a private residence until Harrowells the solicitors (established in York in 1908) occupied it in 1985 and the adjacent Ryedale Court shopping centre was built and opened. The tree on the roundabout was planted for the Coronation of Edward VII in 1902. The farm on the corner of York Road and The Village was sensibly called York Road Corner Farm; it was demolished in 1929 to make way for Norbryte House which accommodated the post office. One of Haxby's casualties in the Second World War, as recorded by John Wright, was seventeen year old Kenneth Cornelius from Hilbra Avenue. He was on the HMS *Royal Oak* when it was sunk at Scapa Flow by a U-Boat and died with 882 other sailors, one of whom was Arthur Long, his friend, from Chestnut Avenue in New Earswick. Kenneth's father was manager of Samuel's the jewellers in Coney Street; both the boys worked at Rowntree's before the war.

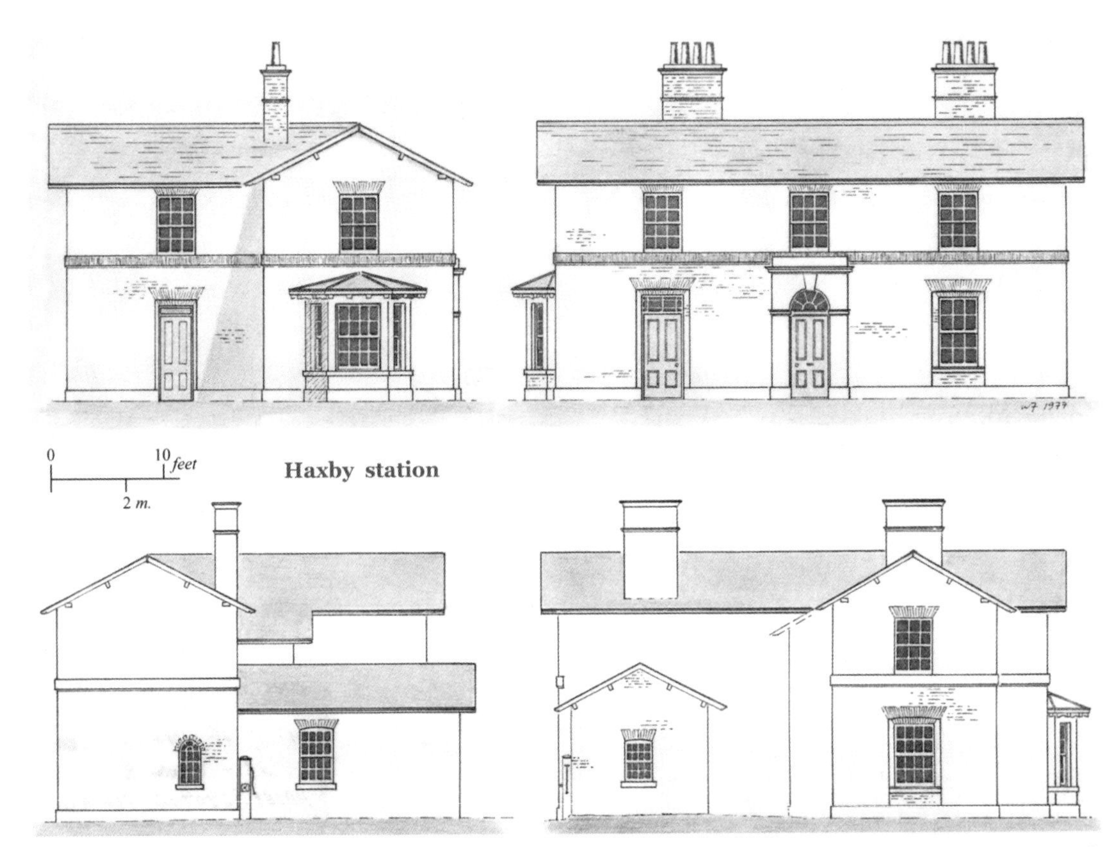

The prospect of a new station in Haxby has become something of a pipedream for those residents who were looking forward to the innocent pleasure, and environmentally sound habit, of getting the train to and from York. It has become mired in the usual self-serving politics at local and national level and will probably never see the light of day, despite the council's worthy huffing and puffing about changing residents' attitude towards car use.

These elevations, drawn up by Bill Fawcett show (clockwise from top left), platform frontage, facade to road, south elevation with gables of kitchen and platform range in foreground; west elevation with one storey kitchen in foreground. Haxby Station was on the York to Scarborough Line and was opened in July 1845 by the York and North Midland Railway. It closed on 22nd September 1930. Bradshaws timetable for summer 1927 shows fifteen trains in each direction on a weekday with two on a Sunday. Trains plied between York and Flaxton railway station; a number were operated by a bus mounted on rail wheels. The initial rail bus was first put into service in 1922 and was based on the road buses operated by the North Eastern Railway (NER) in the Durham area. An additional driving position was fitted to the back and additional doors were fitted in the centre of the bus. The bus could seat 26 passengers and was numbered 110.

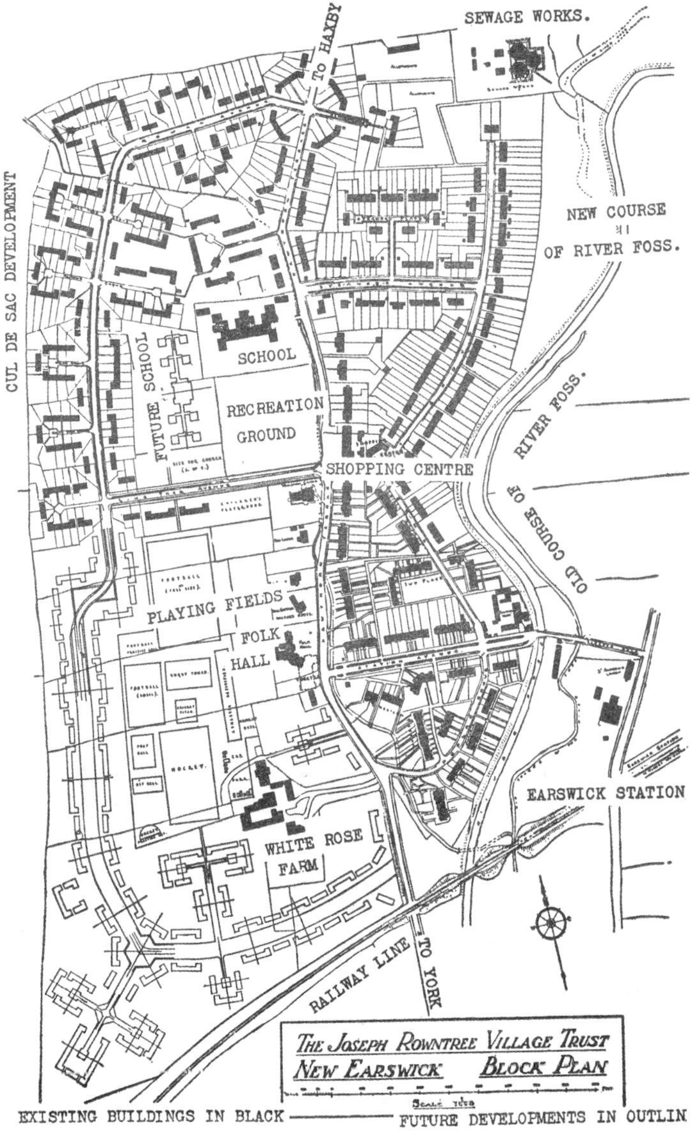

New Earswick: The Edwardian Garden Village

Many people would agree that one of the pinnacles of Joseph Rowntree's social reform lay in the Trusts he established and the garden village that was New Earswick. In 1904 he emulated the Cadbury's when he established three of the four Trusts that live on today: the Social Service Trust, the Charitable Trust and the Village Trust. The Trusts were always intended to be dynamic in that the work they did moved with and were adapted to the times. The beneficiary of the Village Trust was the model garden village that was to become New Earswick, or 'The New Estate' as it was often known .

The simple aim of the Village Trust was to provide the average worker on a wage of about 25 shillings per week with a new type of house that was '*artistic in appearance*', clean, sanitary, and ergonomically designed in an environmentally friendly village with social, religious and educational amenities. In other words, a decent place to live which was not a Hungate or a Walmgate slum. At least 10% of the village would be parks or recreation areas, houses would only take up 25% of the land and there would be strips of grass between the roads and footpaths.

Rowntree's deep concern for the welfare of his workers, the research findings and solutions proposed by his son, Seebohm Rowntree, into local poverty and the plight of the urban poor published in Seebohm's ground-breaking *Poverty: A Study of Town Life*, his own Quaker beliefs, Cadbury's achievements at Bournville and the pioneering work on garden cities by Ebenezer Howard which manifested in Letchworth in 1903, Saltaire – Titus Salt's 1851 model village, James Reckitt's Quaker garden village in Hull in 1908, and later aspects of William Lever's Port Sunlight – all of these would have conspired in Joseph's mind to inspire the establishment of New Earswick on a site just minutes away from the Haxby Road factory between the city of York and the village of Haxby. By 1924 the population of New Earswick was about 2,000; 850 (42%) of these people worked for Rowntree.

Left: Barry Parker's plan for the site drawn up after the First World War; originally published in *Joseph Rowntree Village Trust, One Man's Vision: The Story of the Joseph Rowntree Village Trust.*

Builders on the early stages of New Earswick's construction, posing for the camera in the brickworks, now the nature reserve. The two small boys on the right are Wilf Charlton and his cousin; Wilf grew up to run the grocer's in the village. The village was built from bricks which were made in the local brickworks on the outskirts of New Earswick. It closed down in the 1930s and was developed into the nature reserve in 1950.

A typical New Earswick kitchen fire-range – black leaded and steel – with the oven on one side and the water heater on the other. The toilet and the coal hole were outside but this was far preferable to the shared, insanitary privies of Hungate. The first houses had earth closets which were replaced in 1906 with a water system. In 1948 93% of the 530 houses had three bedrooms; one had two and the rest four or five. Bungalows were built for older residents and featured a large room usable either as a living room-cum-bedroom, or as two separate rooms. This versatility gave obvious social advantages and financial benefits in heating costs; they were fitted with alarm bells for emergencies, connected to a qualified nurse's rent-free residence. Socially and environmentally, New Earswick was years ahead of its time.

Western Terrace: the scullery where the baking and the bathing took place; the covered bath is on the right of the picture. The first coppers were brick but gas coppers and gas ovens came later.

New Earswick's first baby was born in 1905 to the Snowden family. George and Herbert (the two young men) pictured here played in the village's first football team formed in 1906. To quote the Joseph Rowntree Foundation: *"In 1905 the first baby born in New Earswick is the youngest of five. Fifty years later, the size of the average family nationally has halved but the number of families has doubled. By 2003, one in four children lives in a one-parent family; single pensioners live in one in seven homes… With its open spaces, three-bedroom houses, gardens and modern Primary School, New Earswick is originally planned with families in mind. But by the twenty-first century the family has changed. 65 per cent of children still live with both their natural parents. But 10 per cent of couples are cohabiting and 10 per cent of children live with a step-parent"*.

The Co-op in Station Avenue on the right, the first shop to be built in the village in 1908. The original post office is next door. Despite the emergence of shops, horse-drawn delivery continued to be important with dairy products coming from Sorensen's twice a day at 7.00 am and 4.00 pm, and from Crompton Farm.

In developing New Earswick, Joseph Rowntree was heavily influenced by Ebenezer Howard's vision of a kind of utopian city: slum free, largely managed and financed by the residents who had a financial interest. Equal opportunity, good wages, entertainment, low rents, beauty, fresh air were the aim and we can recognise all of these factors in Joseph Rowntree's New Earswick. Howard's humanism and progressive vision was influential in other countries too, not least in Germany where the German Garden City Association, *"unseren Deustschen Vettern"*, flourished. The Association embraced Howard's vision, as evidenced by their visit here on 7th July 1909. There is, however, a sinister side to the story. Theodor Fritsch (1852-1933) claimed to be the originator of the garden city concept, anticipating Howard in his 1896 *Die Stadt der Zukunft* (The City of the Future). Fritsch took a highly racist perspective – completely at odds with Howard's – that later contributed to Nazi ideology and made Fritsch something of a prophet of Nazism. Despite the fact that in 1910 German eugenicists were sitting on the board of the GGCA and the long tradition of town planning and architecture being hijacked in the name of racial cleansing and eugenics, the Association rejected Fritsch.

The village carnival was a popular annual event from 1912 to 1952 which involved most of the village with local traders washing their vans and lorries and decking them out with flowers and bunting. The carnival queen had pride of place on one of these. Marquees were erected, there was fancy dress and races were run; tea was served in the maquees. This picture from around 1950 shows a float occupied by (left to right) Malcolm Jackson, Ann Roe, Malcolm Welsh, Marjorie Nixon, Janet Martin, Margaret Rochester, Jean Windass and Joan Regan.

Carnival day in 1910.

A meeting of the Girls' Club in the Folk Hall in 1910. The Hall was built in 1907. Rowntree actively encouraged women to get out of the home and use the many facilities offered there: *"In this country it seems to be the thought that women do not need recreation"* he pondered, citing the example of Germany where it was and still is the norm for families to go out together as families, with the children. The village library opened here in 1908 with the first 100 books donated by Joseph Rowntree. Many social activities were held in the Folk Hall – one of the purposes of which was to offer societies and clubs a place in which to run activities, reflecting the interests of the residents. During the First World War the hall was used to accommodate Belgian refugees. In the late 40s the Hall took 1075 lettings in one year bringing in £710 with highly profitable Saturday night dances proving particularly popular.

The cast of *The Mikado* in the Folk Hall in 1953. The New Earswick Musical Society was founded in 1914 (from the 1912 Choral Society) as the New Earswick Dramatic Society and 96 years later still performs two shows every year, now in the Joseph Rowntree Theatre in Haxby Road. In 1933 the Society had 260 active members and performed a staggering 24 productions – Gilbert and Sullivan plays and operas – one every two weeks. The success of the society helped drive through a new hall with seating for 450, a well-lit stage and dressing rooms in 1935.

The fancy dress party held in Sycamore Avenue and Sycamore Place to celebrate the end of the Second World War. Another function of the Hall was as a place of worship – for all faiths. In time, though, a separate Wesleyan Chapel and a place for Anglican worship were established, although the Society of Friends and Roman Catholics continued to worship at the Hall. In 1917 it was given Quaker Meeting status and a Sunday school followed in 1918. Societies who have used the hall have included the York & District Budgie Society, York Bridge Club, and the York Coronary Support Group.

The secondary school was opened as Joseph Rowntree School in 1942 to cater for 480 children (in classes of 40) of age eleven and above from the village and surrounding area. Agriculture and horticulture played an important role. As with the primary school, it was a model of innovation, taking advice, for example, from the National Institute of Industrial Psychology on ergonomic issues such as ventilation, heating and lighting. The new 21st century (2011) school is a fitting testament to Joseph Rowntree's 20th century vision. Like its predecessor it is innovative: one of the key features is a centre for autistic children offering specialist teaching and care for all children on the autistic spectrum. The photographs on pages 31–34 were originally published in *The Joseph Rowntree School*.

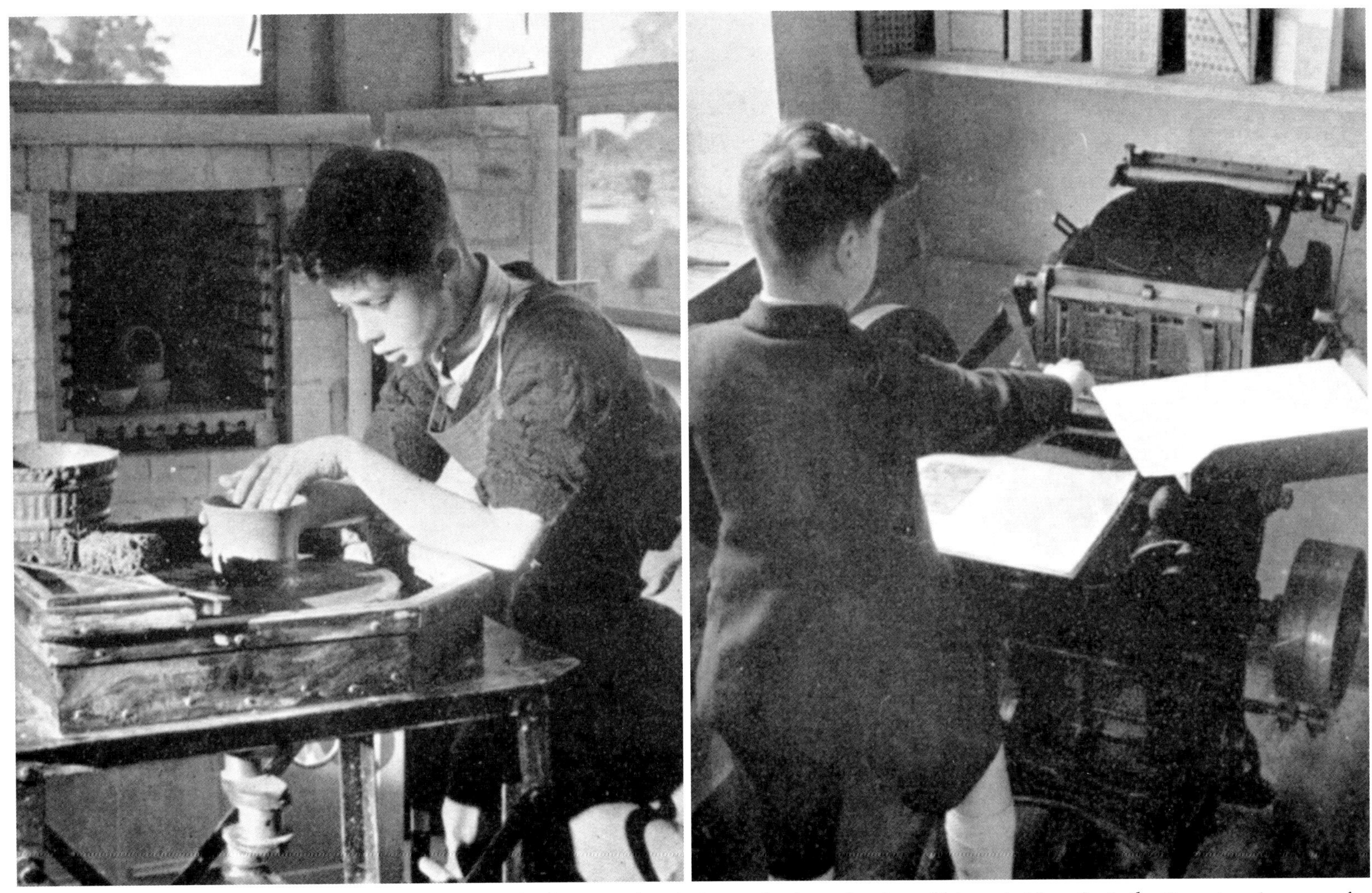

Practical, and in some cases, unusual, subjects were taught, for example printing and print technology. This probably reflects the Rowntrees' concern for the written word and for books, as demonstrated by their involvement in adult education in York. It may also represent a nod towards local industry as Sessions the printers were not very far away in Huntington. Mechanical engineering included the conversion of an old car into a runabout truck. The gym had room for a full-sized boxing ring when required and had a radiogram and piano for use during folk dancing.

The school was designed as an open-air building: innovations included south facing large windows low enough for pupils to see out of when at their desks; they were "*capable of any required degree of opening*" depending on the weather or time of year to provide optimum ventilation and lighting; ceiling heating panels; and "*the long principal corridor* [which] *is slightly curved so as to minimise noise transmission by means of skin friction.*"

The first New Earswick 'school' had opened in the Folk Hall in 1909 after pressure exerted by the Trust on a dilatory local authority and it catered for 25 infants. The first permanent school was built in 1912 for 352 five to fourteen year olds, to save them the trek to Haxby Road School about a mile away. New Earswick School (later New Earswick Elementary School) or The 'Open Air School' as it became known, was a model of enlightenment: boys and girls were taught the same subjects – science teaching, for example, was normally the preserve of boys; there were no high windows – here the full length windows faced south, opened to an extent of eighteen feet and were at head level to maximise natural daylight. Each child had fifteen square feet of floor area affording ample space in between desks – 50% more than was stipulated by the Board of Education then. Class sizes were limited to 30 pupils when at the time in York, classes of between 50 and 60 were the norm; the Trustees paid for an extra teacher to facilitate this. As the school neared completion the influential *Building News* waxed lyrical, highlighting all its features. Many of these were to be replicated in the 1942 secondary school.

Dancing class at the primary school in 1918.

Significantly, it is the school that is at the heart of the village, not, as might be expected, the social and religious centre, the Folk Hall. Joseph Rowntree was always anxious to ensure that education never just meant stuffing children with facts. In his opening address, Joseph Rowntree's views on the prevailing, '*corrupting system in which schools received payment by test result based on a narrow and limiting state curriculum*' – what we now call teaching to test – have an eerily contemporary ring: '*this mechanical system … its general effect was to turn out children who perhaps might pass examinations but whose mental activity was stunted, and who had little capacity for meeting the demands of daily life*'.

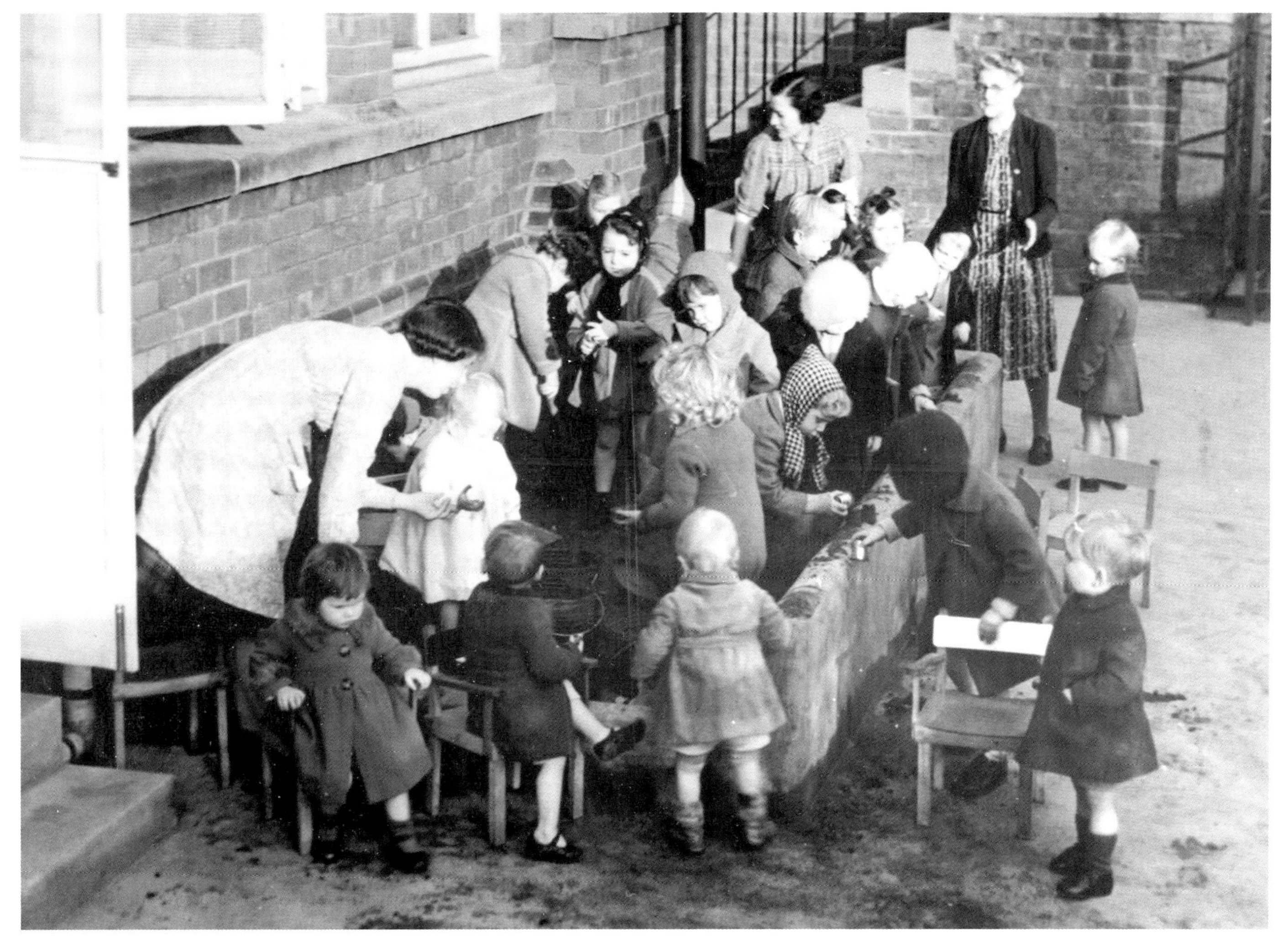

A scene at the nursery school about 1942. The importance of attracting the very best teachers to the Joseph Rowntree Schools was paramount: speaking of the new secondary school, Joseph Rowntree said: '*The most potent influence will no doubt come from the teachers, this will make its self felt in many ways. New Earswick School is coeducational throughout, sewing and cooking will not be neglected for the girls, we want the girls when they grow up to be able to enter marriage with intelligent understanding so that they may be true and helpful companions to their husbands and able wisely to guide the minds of children*'.

Secondary school headteacher Mr. E. Lightowler with pupils in 1944. In November 2009 a time capsule containing a school uniform, a prospectus and dried pasta was buried by Year 11 pupils under a paving slab at the entrance to the new school.

A woodwork class at Joseph Rowntree School in 1944. The school was officially opened on 7th July 1942 by Rab Butler. Total number of pupils was 480, with class sizes of 40. It covered 14 acres (57,000 m²) and was built in what was known as West Huntington Park. The school prided itself on teaching mainly practical and less academic subjects. Initially the school was somewhat untraditional and informal, with no exams. School life was less structured than in most other schools, more laissez-faire and consonant with the Rowntree vision of humanitarian fairness and concord.

The clock on the cupola was donated by Joseph Stephenson Rowntree. The weather vane shows a Quaker reading to two children. The opening ceremony, attended by local dignitaries led by Joseph Rowntree, attracted a number of suffragettes who threw bricks through the windows; Miss Violet Key Jones jumped on the running board of Sir Walter Worsley's car and went on to the Folk Hall to scatter pamphlets urging *"Votes for Women."*

A view of the Co-op. Other shops in the 1930s included Howard's haberdashery, Mrs Farrell's sweet shop, Ernie Wood's chemist, Fred Wiley the cobbler, the Co-op butchers, Burrell's bakers and Coning's wet fish shop.

Earswick Railway Station was on the now defunct York to Beverley Line. It opened in October 1847 and closed in November 1965. In 1911 7,867 tickets were sold from the station catchment area of 1461, which is a mere 21 passengers or so a day; the main use, though, was for industry: 517 tons of bricks (the principal goods) were shipped in 1911 while in 1913 ten wagons of livestock, mainly cattle, were loaded. In its heyday in the 1930s, sidings served the Clarence Leather Works, Ebor Timber and Eborcraft. The large building in the background is Hall's Tannery. The only remaining evidence of the station is the aptly named Flag and Whistle pub and the signal which now occupies the site. The station buildings were demolished in 1971 and the platforms removed in the mid 1970s.

The 1904 White Rose Dairy was the inspiration of Seebohm Rowntree who established the dairy to ensure the provision of clean milk to village residents in the knowledge that contaminated milk was a factor in the high infant mortality rate. To do this he brought in a Dane, Wilfred Sorensen (known locally as Oslo – the capital of Norway!), from the Manchester Pure Milk Co., bought some land for him to build a farm on and develop a herd. For the time, unusually high levels of hygiene were adopted, the milk was filtered and cooled to destroy bacteria.

Ice cream in Chestnut Grove in 1936. The vendor is PB Dairies from Bootham in York. Nearby Chestnut Avenue epitomized the decidedly green ethos of the village: tree lined, virtually traffic free avenues which were, and still are, pleasant to live and play in; the avenues and closes were named after trees.

The Red Lodge pictured in 1921. The Lodge, originally a hostel for single women, including teachers at the primary school, was demolished in 1976. The present building dates from 1976 and is a 65 room retirement housing development. Communal facilities focus on maintaining residents' independence and include dining for residents and guests; lounge; library services; hair salon; treatment room; laundry facilities; guest rooms; landscaped gardens. In January 2012 it was announced that the Joseph Rowntree Trust was planning to spend £20m on redeveloping Red Lodge to provide homes fit for the elderly in the 21st century.

Two typical views of Chestnut Avenue (here and on the next page) showing the virtually traffic free play and pedestrian road that it was around 1920. As an example of the innovative nature of the Village Trust, the early streets in New Earswick were a world apart from York's Victorian terraces. Their planning was influenced by the Garden City movement to include gardens, cul-de-sacs, open space and trees. Cars were low priority: in 1904 there were only 23,000 cars on the road in Britain, but over time, car numbers increased massively and New Earswick's streets were redesigned in response.

Nos. 2-14 Chestnut Grove looking towards Ivy Place. After the Second World War, there was demand for new types of housing, not just family homes but flats for single people and 'sheltered housing' for older people. The Red House and Hartrigg Oaks are examples of the latter.

Two photographs of typical living rooms in New Earswick, from the 1940s. These comfortable residences were the direct result of Seebohm Rowntree's findings in *Poverty: A Study in Town Life* (1901). This landmark work shone much-needed light on the shocking living conditions people endured in dark, overcrowded and unsanitary housing. The 1901 Census confirms this: 8% of the population of England and Wales lived in such homes. Many working-class houses did not have their own piped water supply and few had bathrooms. Only 2% of houses were connected to mains electricity in 1910.

There was considerable rivalry between the early bus services in the village. The first to arrive was the 'Yellow Peril' run by the Northern Motor Utilities in the 1920s, but only as far as the Rowntree factory. 'Cosy Cars' came next, thirty-seater red buses operated by Sherriff & Mennell in competition with the blue buses of the People's Bus Service.

Lights at Nig

Written by Clare Helen Welsh

Collins

We need light to see at night ...

... but too much light can be bad.

Moths feed at night.

They see lights and forget to feed.

Bugs think lights are the moon.

They gather near lights.

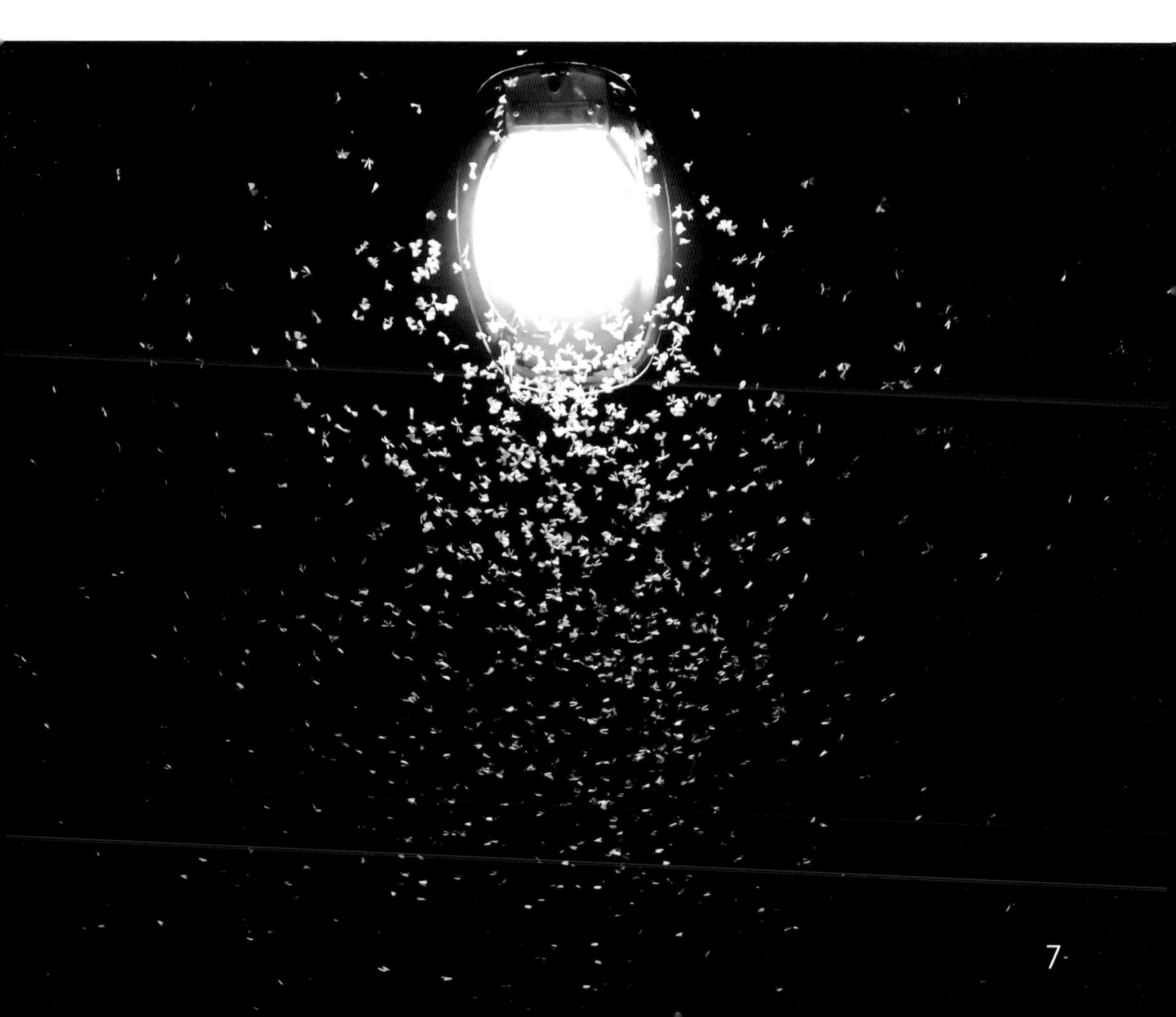

Bats and owls might look for bugs near lights.

This robin thinks the light is morning.

Darker is better for moths, bats and robins ...

... and us too!

Lights at night

Review: After reading

Use your assessment from hearing the children read to choose any GPCs, words or tricky words that need additional practice.

Read 1: Decoding

- On page 8, ask the children to practise finding long vowel sounds. Ask: Which word has the /or/ sound? (***for***) Repeat for:
  short /**oo**/(***look***)   /ow/ (***owls***)
  - Turn back to page 6 and 7. Can they find the /er/ and long /oo/ sounds? (***gather***, ***moon***)
- Model reading page 4 aloud slowly but fluently. Ask the children to read page 5 in a similar way. Say: Can you blend in your head silently when you read these words?

Read 2: Prosody

- Demonstrate reading pages 12 and 13, asking the children to follow in their books, and to look out for the punctuation.
- Did they notice out how you paused at the comma? Say: See how the comma separates two things in a list. Point out how you used extra expression for the exclamation **... and us too!**
- Ask the children to read the pages. Do they respond to the punctuation?

Read 3: Comprehension

- On page 7, point to **They**. Ask: What is meant by "they" here? (*bugs*) Ask the children to look back at the previous page if they are unsure.
- Talk about the children's experiences of lights at night. Do lights wake them up? Do they sleep better in the dark?
- Ask: What sort of lights are bad for moths and bugs? (e.g. *electric lights*) In what way are they different to moonlight? (e.g. *they are unnatural, brighter, confusing*)
- Look at pages 14 and 15, and talk about how information books usually have photographs. Discuss why. (e.g. *they show facts*)
  - Ask the children to chat with a friend and think of a fact for each picture.
  - Prompt with questions, such as: Do you remember what the moth does at night? (*It feeds at night.*)